# NAOMI STOLTZFUS

# Answers for a Happy Family Life

*How to Better Understand Yourself and Your Child in Parenting*

*Copyright © 2024 by Naomi Stoltzfus*

*All rights reserved. No part of this publication may be reproduced, stored or transmitted in any form or by any means, electronic, mechanical, photocopying, recording, scanning, or otherwise without written permission from the publisher. It is illegal to copy this book, post it to a website, or distribute it by any other means without permission.*

*Naomi Stoltzfus asserts the moral right to be identified as the author of this work.*

*First edition*

*ISBN: 979-8-218-49761-3*

*This book was professionally typeset on Reedsy. Find out more at reedsy.com*

# Contents

| | | |
|---|---|---|
| *Preface* | | iv |
| 1 | Being a Happy Parent | 1 |
| 2 | Understanding Our Children's Needs | 7 |
| 3 | How Our Marriage Affects Our Children | 19 |
| 4 | Children Are Teachable | 27 |
| 5 | Repetition | 37 |
| 6 | Teaching our Children How to Connect with God Within... | 40 |
| 7 | What is Manipulation? | 44 |
| 8 | What is the Difference? | 52 |
| 9 | How Often Do We Hurt Our Children Unconsciously? | 57 |
| 10 | Creating Harmony in The Home | 61 |

# Preface

Hi to all who read this book,

I am a mother to 3 boys and 3 girls. Three years ago, my husband and I left our Amish culture and community in search of FREEDOM. Freedom from religious rules, mostly. But it went a lot deeper, as we realized we have a lot of healing and reprogramming to do too. We discovered very few people actually find true freedom. Freedom from pain, heartache, pressure of what others think, and freedom from past mistakes, failures, and our programmed minds.

We wanted freedom for our children, so they can live their lives to their fullest potential. We wanted to have our children's respect, so we don't need to control them. So we searched and questioned. And we went through many hardships, of which we have learned some of our most valuable lessons.

My desire is to share the insights and discoveries with you to give you hope and inspire you to live your greatest life.

In this book, I have included myself in with the rest of you, because I am still learning and will keep learning as long as I live. I learned as I wrote and I am still practicing what I have written. I am not a perfect Mother, but I enjoy my children more than I used to and our life has become so much better as we heal and change. It is rich with valuable experiences.

Our first son died in 2013 at 15 mo. old, then we were blessed with another son a year later in 2014, then 3 daughters and 2 more sons. My husband wears an artificial leg, due to deformities at birth and now our 3 yr old son has the same deformity and is in the process of getting his first artificial leg. This same boy also had open heart surgery to fix his large heart murmur when he was 9 mo. old. He is now an active, healthy boy, and we are so grateful to have him! Our youngest son is normal, and starting to walk soon as his first birthday rolls around.

We have moved 11 times in the 13 years of our marriage and currently live in the beautiful mountains of West Virginia.

We went from being really strict with our oldest children, to no rules at all after we left our controlled, structured lifestyle behind. We discovered that having no rules did not work either, so we kept searching for a happy medium where we can all be happy and experience joy with each other.

I asked my children numerous times what they think we should do, when we were dealing with a certain issue that I was at loss with. It continues to amaze me what simple solutions they came up with, and how well they work. Together we have created a lifestyle we all love and now we are ready to move forward, sharing our discoveries with you and inspire you to live your greatest life! Here you are with raw material and no professional editors involved. I just wrote it as if I was writing to my sister or best friend in authenticity and realness. I invite you to pick out the best, put it to test, and leave the rest.

This is my first book, and I did it by myself, so don't expect perfection. I want to write more books of our life story, so know that this is only the beginning.

My prayer is that you can experience A-ha moments as you read and discover answers for your life's puzzles as we navigate onward towards a brighter future for ourselves, our children, our communities, and all over the world. Sending you love, Naomi

Stoltzfus

# 1

# Being a Happy Parent

To do what is best for our family will only be possible if we can find harmony within ourselves.

To do that, we need to,[1] #1, let go of the past. #2 live in the present. #3 enjoy the moments. and #4 work at finding our true passion, which is doing the thing we truly enjoy... that thing we could be doing all day long and not get tired of it... That thing that fulfills us and brings value to humanity.

#1 How do we let go of the past?

First, we must realize where our past has brought us and what kind of life we have created so far, whether it was consciously or unconsciously. Which, most likely was unconsciously and not our fault at all.

But if we do not find ways to change it, we will create more of our future the same way. Nobody else can do this for us. Our future is up to us. We just need to become aware that we really do have choices in this world, and it really matters what we think and do about it.

---

[1]

Once we become aware of what makes us sad or unhappy, then we can find answers on how to fix that. And once we know what really excites and inspires us, and brings us joy, then we can do more of that. Being aware of our emotions, whether happy or unhappy can give us a lot of answers and direction on what we want to create in our life that would be a blessing to others.

The emotions we have now, most likely come from past experiences, whether happy or unhappy, and how we have been programmed to think. And when we become aware of our emotions, we can probably see patterns, where some things seem to go around in endless cycles, always coming back to the starting point. Once we make enough positive changes in our life to disrupt the cycle and start new behavior patterns, then our life will start to shift. And then we can see our life changing for the better.

To reprogram our brain and think differently than it did, we want to imagine and write out the new story of our life that we want to live in the future.

Step#1 Imagine a life that would make you happy...... What would you do that you would totally enjoy? Where would you live, so that you could be excited to get out of bed in the morning? With what kind of people would you like want to live life with and create values that humanity needs? Who do you want to be inspired by? How would this kind of life you just imagined, make you feel? When would you like to live this kind of life? 1 year from now, 2 years, 5 years, 10 years?

Once you know what you want to achieve in life, write it down and then you are ready for step #2.

Step #2. Start feeling the excitement and thrill of living the kind of life you just imagined. How happy would you be? Just feel how wonderful it would be to give your children the kind of life you would have loved as a child. Children deserve the happiest life we can provide for them. And it is worth making good changes for their sake, and us, too. Our children can be our biggest reason to change our life for the better. If we can change our life, we are creating a better future for the next generation, and for the world, and change the course of history. It may not be easy, but it will be worth it!

Step#3. Alright, now that we are all excited about the future life we want to create, how do we feel? Most likely we want it now and are trying to come up with ideas and ways to make this ideal life come about. Worrying about the "how" can be frustrating, which will only hinder us, so just let go of that pressure and let the ideas and inspirations flow. Just relax and know that once your brain gets told often enough what you want, you can start believing it. And when you feel the excitement daily, then your brain can come up with new and inspiring actions to take.

Step#4. The next step is important. Be grateful for what you already have. Being grateful brings your happiness level up, which helps you 'feel' how your future life will feel and thus helps your brain believe that your dreams are possible. And, be grateful for the future dream and lifestyle, as if it has already happened, which will further trick your brain into believing that it is possible. Once you can believe it, you can achieve it. Another important thing is to be grateful for,is the hard things in your life. Anything that is hard to be grateful for. The only way that you can do that, is when you can accept what it is and believe that something good can come out of it. And, that things happen for a reason and there is a lesson to be learned, which we can someday treasure.

Step#5. Now, once you are at peace with your vision and are excited and happy, your brain can now produce ideas and inspired actions to take to achieve it. Once it believes that this vision is possible, you are on the way to making your dreams a reality. You will encounter obstacles along the way but keeping your vision in front of you and staying grateful for the obstacles, you will get the strength you need to keep going and overcome all limitations. Now make sure you know the difference between inspired action and forced action. Taking inspired action means going in the flow of excitement and harmony. It can mean doing something uncomfortable or risky, but it should bring thrill and joy. Usually, it does not mean doing something you hate and must force yourself to do it.

If we can do these 5 steps daily for 3 weeks, we will see a change in our life.

Changing our current life for the life we dream of, is not easy, but it can be an exciting journey. Do not expect things to change overnight, lest you be disappointed and discouraged. Give yourself grace and room to grow and change.

Change brings chaos. Just accept that. It is okay. Think for example: When we change our furniture around in our house, we don't just change it around, for lo and behold, when we move something around, what do we see? We see dirt, dust, and 'who knows what' under and behind furniture. Especially if it has not been moved in a while. So, then we clean there first, before we put something else there, which can be a lot of work. And it can be quite chaotic with things out of order, but how nice it is, once everything is arranged in a new and clean fashion.So, remember, changing is chaotic and that is okay.

To truly be able to let go of our past, we must see what it is, then be willing to "let it go" and make a change. When we hold on to the life we are used to, we go on creating more of the same.

Next, we want to see what it is like to live in the present

moment. How can we enjoy the 'now' moments? Let us think about the morning moments, when we are making breakfast for ourselves and our family. A child comes to us right when they wake up and want us to look at them. The child wants recognition and love. To be seen and talked to. We are the first person and the most important person in their life at this moment. These moments are so precious and fleeting and all too soon they will not need our "Good morning" and our hug as they grow to adulthood. These moments are for us to enjoy briefly as they slip through our fingers like sand. If we do not enjoy these moments as they pass by us, when will we ever get a second chance? This child we have now, will not stay small and the present moments are the only moments we have.

Another way to enjoy the moments together as a family, is to sit around the table to eat meals. Looking at each other's faces and hearing what the little people have to say, can prove to be interesting. These are moments are to be enjoyed and treasured.

And think of the moments when our toddler or preschooler wants to help us with something. It is easy to feel too busy or bothered by their little requests to do something with us, but that is when we miss the present moments. It may not always be appropriate to let them help, but a lot of times we can, if we really want to.

If we let them help us when they are little, they will gladly help us when they are bigger, and we really want them to help us. Especially when we make it fun and praise them for their contributions.

Going outside with them a bit, always brightens my day as a mom. There is something about going out in the fresh air and watching nature that just works wonders for me. And it is so exciting for little children! The big outdoors where there is no end to new things to discover and do. Children love activities, playing games, just anything to make use of their energy. And it makes it even more fun when we help them play. It reduces stress for us bigger people to take time to play with our little ones and enjoy the moments.

When we spend time with them when they are little, they will naturally want to be with us when they get older.

Now for us to be happy enough to enjoy these moments with our dearest people on earth, we need to become the best version of ourselves. We need to discover our true passion. The thing we can do all day and love every minute. The thing that brings us joy and makes us feel excited about life.

How can we feel joyful when we just do not feel happy? How can we enjoy the present moment when we are barely able to scrape by? It can be difficult and feel impossible, but once we learn the art of gratitude, things can change for the better.

Remember, our current life is a result of our past programming and is not our fault, but it is up to us to change it. It is up to each of us to create the life that brings joy to ourselves and to the world.

# 2

# Understanding Our Children's Needs

First, we will look at our children's physical needs which are

#1. Food

#2. Water

#3. Air

#4. Sunshine

#5. Exercise

#6. Supplemental Nutrition

Physical needs are simple because we all have them and are used to them. But here are some pointers on why they are important and how they affect our children's behavior. And it is true for adults as well.

#1. Food

When we feed our children nutrient dense foods like fresh fruits and vegetables, grass-fed meats, and properly prepared grains, their bodies can grow and develop naturally and function in a normal healthy way. A healthy child is a happy child.

Do we expect our children to feel good and happy when their bodies do not have what they need to grow naturally? How can we expect them to have what they need to grow, when we feed them mostly sugar, starches, and fats that are not healthy? (which is what processed foods are made of, not to mention the colorings, preservatives, and artificial flavors that are added)

The best way we can ensure that they get healthy food is when we grow and prepare it ourselves. Which is something not everyone can do with the lifestyle they live. So, the second-best option would be to get fresh food from someplace local whom we can trust. A local organic farmer that does not use pesticides and GMO's. Buying fresh is so much better than shipped foods. And if our jobs keep us from feeding our precious little ones and ourselves in a healthy way, it may be good to check into a different way to make income.

Lots of children do not like fruits and vegetables. Maybe it is because they never had anything fresh out of a garden. It does taste different! And when children help plant a garden and help harvest the food, they will be much more excited about eating it. Especially when they are included in preparing the food they picked. Teaching children at an early age to prepare food can reduce a mother's workload in later years. Because the time will come when they grow big enough to help and do things by themselves. It may not be easy to let them help when they are little, but it will be worth it. It does not have to be all easy. It can be hard to be a young mom, trying to be a good one, but it will also be hard when we are not good moms. Choose your hard. Being a good parent is not for the faint of heart.

It may be hard to make sure our children and ourselves are fed properly, but it is also hard to take care of unhealthy children or unmanageable children. Choose your hard. And try to enjoy the hard moments, because someday we may realize that the challenging times were also good times.

#2. Water

Water is so important for our children's health as well as our own health. Drinking sodas or juice instead of water results in an overdose of sugar. Which then leads to many, many problems. Sugar pulls the minerals out of your body. Minerals which your body needs to stay healthy. Now natural sugars are okay in moderation when your child is not dealing with diabetes. Our bodies need some sugar to survive, but it should come from fruits, honey, maple syrup, and in ways our body is able to use it. Refined sugar and high fructose corn syrup is what is hard on our systems.

Our bodies are made of mostly water, so it is important to replenish it daily so it can function properly. And if we, as parents, have a habit of drinking plenty of fresh water, it will be easy for our children to drink water, too. And if we give them water regularly when they are toddlers, they naturally want water when they are older.

It is easy to not realize that our child may be thirsty when they are unhappy, especially when they are not talking yet. It is easy to assume the child may be hungry, or anything else, but a lot of times children are thirsty, and we do not think about that. I, as a mother, still need to remind myself to ask my children first if they want a drink of water before I offer them food. And I like to try and give my little children a drink of water every time I get a drink.

Humans die of thirst sooner than they die of hunger, because water is more important than food.

#3. Fresh air

#4. Sunshine

#5. Exercise

These three go nicely together and can all be obtained outside. Space to run and play outdoors is crucial for a child's normal development. Being shut up inside all day with bright screens to look at does not fill this need that human beings have, especially children, to feel healthy and normal.

Children benefit from the sense of freedom that comes from running with the wind in their ears, breathing in big gasps of fresh air, and laughing and screaming with everything they have. Pure sunshine provides Vitamin D and strengthens their immune systems. So does playing in the dirt and mud. Connecting with Mother Nature at it's best. And it is good for us adults to do the same. Feel the sense of freedom and connection to the source we come from, the energy we feel in the air, just like the little innocent children. Let them teach us how to connect to our real mother. Doing little things like this with our little ones enhances happy, healthy living, and is bonding as well.

That is another reason why growing our food is so much fun, because it gets us to play in the dirt. And it gives us a worthwhile reason to go outside and do something with our children.

#6. Supplemental Nutrition

Nowadays it is hard to ensure that we get enough nutrition we need just from our foods, even when we grow our own or buy from a good source. Because if minerals are not in the soil, they will not be in the plants and food that grow out of that soil. And many of our garden soils are depleted.

So, to ensure my children get all the nutrition they need, the best way is to supplement with a good, trusted program of some kind. Doing research is important because there are a lot of low-quality pills etc. out there. Finding a good quality program is worth it.

We personally went through financial struggles at times where we could not buy nutrition for our family, and the difference was very noticeable when we could afford nutrition again. We have seen it make a difference in our life, and that is why we see it as important.

And it was amazing how much reserve our children had because they had plenty of nutrition as babies and young children. Through our period of lack, the reserve they had, helped them survive through it all without much suffering.

What I am trying to point out is that having been built up with nutrition before the hard times, saved our children from suffering undernourishment.

Next, we will go over the emotional needs which are
  #1. Relatedness
  #2. Competence
  #3. Autonomy
These three are the main ones we will discuss, so let us start with #1

#1. Relatedness

This means connection. It is the knowing that we are connected to someone who loves us unconditionally. That, whatever happens, someone will care and that no matter how many blunders we make, someone will still love us. It makes us feel safe, no matter where we go. It means we are never alone, no matter where we may go, or what we get inspired to do.

It means someone believes in us and trusts us. And it gives us the ability to trust others and believe in ourselves. It makes us feel secure.

It means we have someone to empathize with us, which means we have someone who cares about us.

The opposite of relatedness is rejection. Sadly, many of us know what rejection feels like. Maybe we do not even realize we suffer from rejection. When we feel in the way, have low self-esteem, can't trust anyone, feel unworthy, feel alone, or feel like nobody cares, then it could be that we are suffering from some form of rejection.

Rejection is one of the worst emotional traumas we, as human beings, can feel, because we are created to connect with each other. We are not created to feel happy existing separately. Being cut off from each other is the same level of pain as cutting of a part of our physical body. Because humans co-exist as a body. One part has this to do, another part has that to do.

Yes, it is possible to go on living without that part, but sadly we are not whole anymore and there will always be a scar. And we just cannot do alone what we can do together. Living separately, is like being crippled.

Thankfully, healing is possible, and life can be restored, but it takes time and a lot of loving ourselves and understanding the pain we feel when we have been rejected. Once we heal, we will once again be able to trust other people and live vibrantly.

So how do we as parents, ensure that our own children do not feel rejected by us? We may be unconsciously making them feel rejected by our habits or ways of living and doing life. The ways of generations before us may not always be the right way or the best way. Maybe there are things we do on a regular basis that makes our children feel rejected, and then we wonder why they behave like they do. What if we could go back and feel how we felt as a child and what we longed for our parents to do for us? Get the feeling how a child feels or how you felt as a child. And if that is painful, just give yourself a hug and love the past child in you. Remember it is not your or our fault, but it is up to each of us to find answers on how to make it better for our children. And if we do not find answers how to make things better, there is no other option than doing the same our parents have done before us, because that is how we have been programmed and it is the life we are creating for our children if we do not make a change. Lot of times when people do try to do different than their parents, it goes the opposite direction, which can be just as harmful. The main thing is to find the answer to the why's and then find middle ground.

For young children to feel related to someone, they need to be looked at and listened to and talked to. Not just young children, but all children. When they do not get it, they will do anything to get attention. You name it ......Whine, fight, climb on top of things, hurt themselves, interrupt adult conversation, get sick, act like a baby, and so on. It is such a great need they have. When we ignore them with this emotional need, they will feel rejected. And will search for it in other ways that may not be good.

Why do we, as parents, not provide for this need easily? We want to have this connection with our children. So why don't we? This brings us to the point where we need to figure out our life to make TIME for our little ones. Love is spelled T-I-M-E in little people's eyes. If our children and family are important to us, we will prioritize and make time for them.

Now we may be asking ourselves, "How can we make time for them if we do not even have time for ourselves?"

Do we love and respect ourselves enough to figure out how to live a joyful life and become responsible for our own happiness and time, or do we let others tell us how to live our life and then whine and grumble about it in victim mentality? Is our need for relatedness still so great that we want to get approval and be "good enough" in other's eyes, so we do not get rejected? So we can feel connected and loved by other people? Then we fall into the trap of being what other people think we should be, instead of who we are created to be, which can bring a lot of misery.

If we do not have people in our lives who love us unconditionally like we need to be loved and our need to relate to someone in a healthy way is not met, then what can we do?

Then the only person who can make sure we get loved, is ourselves. When we can connect with our inner being, our soul, and let ourselves be loved by who we are inside, then we can find happiness and contentment and healing within.

Once we find our inner spark and love and joy, then old things fall away and a new you emerges, and a new life begins. The healing journey is not easy, but we all need to be healed and there is no use thinking it is too hard, because it is also hard to not be healed and live in pain. Choose your hard.

#2. Competence

We all need competence. We all need challenges to overcome, which makes us feel fulfilled and triumphant and vibrant. We have a need to grow, expand and learn new things, no matter what our age is. Learning new things keep us young. People get old quick when life becomes stagnant and boring.

Children, especially, want to master things and try doing things by themselves, like putting their socks on alone, or getting a drink by themselves, or whatever they get inspired to do. They want to help us do things and learn how. Their life is full of new things to do and see and it is one of the reasons children are happier people. Just because they are learning so many new things.

For us, as human beings, living on planet earth, there are always new things to learn and create. Only once we feel like we live in a little box with the lid on, does our life become stagnant and boring. Or like a glass ceiling that keeps us from rising. And we may not even realize we cannot rise, or that we have an invisible ceiling. It is necessary to become aware and learn what is holding us back from freedom and prosperity. Then once we know what bounds us, then it is up to us to break out of it.

Learning and growing and overcoming builds confidence, self-esteem and happiness in all of us.

It is so easy for us, as parents, to be too busy, too stressed, or too tired to let our little ones help us. It is easier and quicker to do things by ourselves. But once we realize the value we are providing for them by letting them help, then it becomes worthwhile.

And another value of letting them help is, soon we will have helpers that can help us in many little ways, which will make our workload easier. When we are always too busy to let them help when they are young, they will lose interest. And once they get big enough to be a big help, they will not want to anymore.

And another bonus that comes with letting our children help us is, it takes a lot less toys. Helping bigger people do something can be even more enjoyable than toys, and here are some reasons why. First.... Doing something with someone they love fills the need for relatedness. They feel connected to us when we do things together. Second reason is...Doing something in the real world is more fun than just imagining it. The actual 'doing' of creating something is more fun than dreaming or talking about it.

Did you ever notice how quickly a new toy becomes stale and boring? At first it is new and therefore exciting. Because children are constantly growing and changing, they constantly need new things to experience, to match that growth. And we, as parents, who have done something so many times, forget how exciting it was the first time we did it. And we have a lot of things to teach our growing children that may be boring to us now. But it can be exciting when we see their excitement in the moment.

Everything we know we can pour into their cups, little by little, as their capacity to learn expands. Just seeing their enjoyment makes it worth all the bother and extra time we put into letting them help us. And they enjoy it even more when they can see us getting pleasure out of it as well.

Remember it is up to us to raise a new generation that is better than before, which will eventually change the world. As the old saying goes, "The hand that rocks the cradle is the hand that rules the world"

#3. Autonomy

This is our need to make decisions for ourselves. To be independent and to be our own unique person. To fill this need we will need the freedom to choose.

When this need is filled, respect for ourselves and others come naturally. So does co-operation. We, as human beings, naturally want a peaceful, respectful and co-operative life.

Giving our children the freedom to choose is respecting them at a deep level. It tells them we realize they are a unique person. Someone that only they know about.

So, when we want them to do something that needs to be done, like taking a nap for example: Asking them if they want to sleep in their bed or our bed, gives them the feeling that they have the freedom to choose, even though they are doing what we want them to do. This is what we call options within limits. Another example is: What time do we want to clean up? This gives them space to make a decision, and therefore, the feeling associated with cleaning up makes them feel important.

Giving our children orders and commands takes away their ability to think for themselves. If they are trained to only obey and always follow and be subject to someone bigger, they become followers instead of leaders. Being a follower can be dangerous, because anyone can become our leader, and if it is not a good leader, then woe to the follower. And if they do not learn how to lead themselves, think for themselves, or be their own person, they will have a hard time as an adult, to find the confidence they need to succeed in life. Many parents who have been very strict with their children when they were young, now wonder why their adult children continue struggling and needing them. As adults, their children should now be able to support them, their aging parents.

Letting children make mistakes when they are little is far less expensive than keeping them walking in order so much, that when they finally do get to the age of making decisions for themselves, their mistakes get a lot more costly, if they can even make decisions at all.

People starting to make decisions at 18 or 21 have much bigger mistakes to make as they learn, than a 2 or 3 yr. old, or any age growing up. Because when we face reality, at some point in time, children need to learn to make their own decisions. Parents cannot protect their children forever. We have a limited amount of time to prepare our children to face the world, and that is when they are small enough to listen what we have to say and not yet old enough to close their ears and hearts to what we have to say. The sweet spot is as soon as they are old enough to comprehend what we are saying or when they can question us about a certain subject. Those questions are our golden moments. It may be the only chance we get. They may never ask us that same question again. And when they are little, they listen to instructions a lot better, therefore they make less mistakes. Once children think they know better than their parents, then it becomes hard for the parent to teach or advise the child.

Now, just because children can make decisions on their own,

does not mean they do not need someone to lead and guide them. Little children feel safer when they have authority above them to keep them from dangers as they grow. That is what parents are for. Children still need to learn obedience and they need to learn how to respect people that have more experience and knowledge than them, which means to not let little people manipulate everything their way, with no regard for older people. There is a reason why 10-year-olds are not allowed to drive cars. A car would become a dangerous weapon in the hands of a child. Children need to become responsible and trustworthy with little things first while they are still little, so they are ready for the bigger responsibilities, when the time comes.

As we teach our little children to obey us for their own safety, they can realize that it is for their best interest if it is done with love, instead of forceful anger. When children feel respected and listened to, there is less need to rebel. Deep down children know they have rights as a human being, and they deserve to be respected as one. By showing our children respect, they learn how to be respectful people. And when we have a habit of listening to what they have to say, they will love listening to what we have to say, because children are natural conversationalists if they do not get told to shut up when they are beginning to talk. Or, have some other trauma to heal from.

# 3

# How Our Marriage Affects Our Children

Creating an atmosphere where love, joy, and happiness flows, starts at the heart of Father and Mother's relationship.

To have a happy family life in full completeness there must be harmony in the relationship of the parents. We may as well call it a heavenly marriage. How to have a heavenly marriage could be a whole book, but in this chapter we will discuss some tips and facts.

One fact is that if either the mother or the father does not feel happy from deep inside, then the other will not feel truly fulfilled. Marriage is a union that must function as one, yet we each need to be our own unique person and govern our own self. Because if one feels less than the other, there is not harmony. Again, respect for each other is an important thing in a marriage.

Remember this: "All men are created equal."

Just because we have different roles and personalities, does not mean we are lesser or better than the other. Often the woman is dominated by the man because women are deemed as the weaker vessel. How can we, as women, fulfill our potential, if we believe we can only do so much? Just because we may not be as strong physically, does not mean we are not as valuable or important. We need to be equally yoked if we want harmony.

As human beings we each have a need to be valued. We need to feel of worth, to know what true happiness is.

Deep inner happiness comes from being fulfilled and valued. And we need to know that we are of value and that we can produce value for others, so that we can feel valuable.

Everyone wants to be needed by someone and to be of value to someone else. It is important that we matter to someone, and to know that we are not alone. Humanity is created to function as a whole, as one body, yet individually, each person bringing his/her own uniqueness and talents to benefit others. When we can do this, happiness abounds. Especially in a marriage relationship.

Separation works the opposite. Separating ourselves from whomever is hurting us is necessary in order to heal and get a different perspective, but it should not be used to control and manipulate. Separating ourselves from others with an egotistic mindset of 'I am better than you' and to set ourselves apart from the rest because we think they are not good enough, or whatever, is destructive, both to ourselves and others.

The saying, 'Absence makes the heart grow fonder' can be true and healing when both parties go within themselves to heal. But sometimes we need to let go completely of someone who just wants to control us and keep on controlling us. We all need to learn how to govern our own selves and become responsible for our own life and future.

Blaming others will never make the world a better place, but taking responsibility to change ourselves, will make the world a better place.

Even if things may not be our fault, staying in victim mentality will not make a better future for ourselves and our children. It is still up to us to create a better future for the next generations and ourselves. Is it worth our time to wait on others, to become a better person than we were yesterday?

We want to be happy, and we want others to be happy. That is what humanity craves and we do anything we can to find joy in life. We search for joy, and we search for answers on how to feel joyful. As long as we keep thinking that joy comes from something or someone outside of ourselves, then we will always feel empty, because joy comes from within. We need to find out how to get the cap off our fountain, so it can bubble out. Open our doors wide and let the goodness flow out.

Fulfillment brings joy. What do we love to do, that is fulfilling to us? We need to discover what talents we have, then start doing the things that bring value to others. It is what we are created to do. Doing the things we are naturally good at and sharing it with the world is bringing the wealth out from within ourselves and is deeply satisfying and fulfilling, bringing us deep joy that effortlessly bubbles out and no one can quench.

Now the opposite is, when we are just doing what others think we should do and making others successful, instead of ourselves. Then we become subject to their joy, which breeds resentment, unhappiness, anger, and we are unable to rise. Then we cannot understand why we can't find joy in life. And we wonder why we aren't better parents even when we have such good intentions.

When we do the things we are good at, then our work becomes play. We feel joy. We feel happy. And then our happiness and joy flows out of us and overflows unto others. Because our cup is full and running over, we have what it takes to bless others.

Imagine a world where each one of us would be doing what we are good at! Everyone's cup would be running over with abundance! Abundance of Love, Joy, Peace, and Prosperity.

Once we learn how to stand up and govern ourselves, instead of letting other people govern and control us, then the world will become a better place. Remember, all men [and women] are created equal. No one is better than another. No man has the right to control another, because we are born with free will and are all created equally by God.

Obviously, little people need grown-ups to lead them while they are still too small to govern themselves, and they also need us to protect them from danger. But the sooner they can learn how to become responsible for themselves, the better. Us parents are here to teach them and show them how. Children are not ours to keep. They will be in our care only a small percentage of their life, and it is up to us to build a relationship with them while they are little, so they want to stay in our company, even when they do not need us and our advice anymore. If we are too protective, so that we limit them and damage their ability to fly when the time comes, they may resent us, and just feel like slipping out from under our control.

Over-protectiveness is a form of control. Even when we do it because we want the best for them, it can still be damaging. Letting go of fears is an inner work that we need to do to be able to discern what is best for our children. When they do get hurt, we need to know that our bodies are designed to heal again. And when they get hurt, they learn not to do that again, and it makes them resilient and responsible for their own safety. How does a child experience real life if we always shield them? Does a child ever learn how to walk without falling? Does a child ever learn how to ride a bike without falling? Does a child learn how to skate without falling?

Our duty is to be there as they learn, show them the best we can and teach them how to get up again after they fall and try again. It is our duty to cheer them on and inspire them to be adventurous and experience life to the fullest. Or maybe even turn it around and let them teach us how to be adventurous and enjoy life to the fullest.

We are humbled by the fear we have. We have been programmed and conditioned with more fear than necessary, but as we come to understand that all things work together for good, then fear becomes irrelevant, and all things become possible. God is here with all the answers inside us. We only need to learn how to connect to our inner wisdom and guidance, and we will find all the answers we will ever need. The answers may not always be what we expect, so we need to stay awake and aware to the world around us and keep learning with open hearts. Once we find the answer to our question, it is up to us to take action and make the changes that are necessary.

When we can make the necessary changes needed in our life to have a harmonious marriage, then we can be the prime example for our little children. They will be able to see firsthand what a happy marriage looks like. And since children are good imitators, they will strive to have marriages like they see their parents enjoy.

As they grow up and choose their life partner, we need to step back and let them form a new union and live out their life choices. Many a mother-in-law has ruined their child's marriage because she could not let go when it was time. Because she thought this newcomer must now conform to the family's way of living and believing.

For a marriage to blossom into something beautiful, both husband and wife need to merge their beliefs into a new union. For that to happen, both need to let go of their parents to create this new version.

Us parent's time to train our children is when they are little and by the time they are old enough to marry, we should have them completely ready to fly the nest and fly on their own. Our parenting role will then be completed for that child. At that age children become completely responsible for their decisions and actions, unless we have not taught them responsibility and still try to shoulder everything for them.

If they have children, they will likely raise them like their parents have raised them, unless they decide to change things and do differently. And as grandparents, we will be free from the responsibility of raising our grandchildren and be able to enjoy them fully if we still have a good relationship with our grandchildren's parents. If we do not have a good relationship with our grandchildren's parents, they have the power to keep our grandchildren away from us. It will be a time of harvest for us, and we will be reaping what we have sowed in our children's hearts when they were little.

Again, the time to be happy is now, the place to be happy is here, and the way to be happy is to make others [and ourselves] happy, and we will have a little heaven down here.

Now is the time to feel the love, look our loved ones in the eyes and say, "I love you" with meaning. Little children are easy to kiss. Teenagers may be a bit more challenging. To let our children see the love between us, as husband and wife, gives them pictures etched in their brains, what love looks like. And they will naturally act it out what they see being done. Same is true the other way around. If our children regularly see us arguing or fighting, they will practice it, too. And once it becomes a habit, either way, then the training is completed. And a habit continues, unless it gets changed, because it gets done without thinking.

Example is a big part in child training and very effective. It works better than strict rules and control. If children have a good example, they become a good example for others. When they are treated with respect, they become respectful to each other, and when they see their parents being respectful to each other, they learn what respect looks like. When they are loved unconditionally and they see their parents love each other unconditionally, they will know what unconditional love is. When they see and hear their parents being grateful to each other and to them, [saying thank-you for the little things and showing appreciation], they will know what gratefulness means.

A great way to see ourselves, is to look at our children for our mirror. They reflect what they see. Since they are of the blood of two parents, they are a mixed-up version of us, who should be functioning as one union. Many times, it is easy to blame the other parent for how the children are becoming, but it is never just one parent's fault or problem. If we want harmony, we need to work together and help each other. Find out what works in-between the differences. If a marriage functions as one, in Love, there would not be any unsolvable problems or issues. When the whole family pulls together in one team, the whole family becomes unity, powerfully moving forward towards a great future, with each person being their own person. This is how we are created to be.

When we can practice this first in our homes with our families, we are creating a new and better version of humanity, sharing the love, and the joy it brings to others, where it can multiply and change the face of Earth.

There is a lot of inner work to be done to achieve this harmonious state of being. We may feel stuck, at where we are in life. We may wonder why we do things the way we do. We may wonder why we react to certain things the way we do. It can all be traced back to how we have been trained and conditioned. But the good news is, our brains can be retrained or reprogrammed. Our brains are still mold-able throughout our life and that is why we can learn new things. It is good to realize that there is still hope to change our life around and make new paths, but it is up to each of us to take responsibility for ourselves and do our inner work and healing. It benefits not only ourselves, but our children, our communities, and the whole world. If we have a desire to change the world, the place to start is within ourselves.

Children thrive in this atmosphere of harmony and have no reason to rebel. They love harmony and peace in their world. When they experience this kind of atmosphere while growing up, it will positively affect them for the rest of their life. And sadly, the opposite is true as well.

If we, as adults, have grown up negatively, then we can see how much it affects our life. Thankfully there is help and healing out there for people who search and want to change their lives around. Our brains can be reprogrammed, but it takes dedication and persistence and a lot of love and patience with ourselves. It is worth it, so we can remove the generational curses, and create a better future for our children.

So let us take heart, my friends, there is hope.

# 4

# Children Are Teachable

Here are four good things to teach to our children:

1. Work ethic
2. Responsibility
3. Teamwork
4. Creativity

One important thing to remember is: To be a good teacher means to have mastered the skills that we are teaching.

If we have not mastered these four skills, then we must learn and master them ourselves before trying to teach them, or else let the children teach us. They may surprise us with their wisdom and knowledge they get from within themselves, and it is good if we can humble ourselves and learn from them, because children are great teachers.

Again, example plays a big part in teaching. Showing is easier and more effective than telling. Explaining is important, but too much talking and not enough doing, makes it confusing and boring for children. They love anything fun and happy. All these four things should be taught in a fun way for them to have a lasting positive effect.

There are also more things to teach our children, but these four are important, so let's start with #1.

#1. Work Ethic

There are two different kinds of 'work ethic'.

1. Internal motivation, which makes a good 'work ethic' and
2. External motivation, which makes a bad 'work ethic'.

Internal motivation is when we want to work, and external motivation is when we must work.

Both can be trained in children.

To teach children internal motivation, we need to work with them and show them the value of why and what we are doing. When we include them as someone that has value to offer, and then praise them for their effort and contribution, it will become a fun experience. And celebrate afterwards for the accomplishment with a reward, or some playtime. Rewarding children for a job well done, is different from bribing them with a reward, to get them to do what we want. Bribing does not create a good 'work ethic'. Bribing destroys internal motivation.

A good 'work ethic' comes with the excitement of the value of the work we do, instead of the reward. Though most times, when people provide value, they get rewarded naturally. This goes for people of all ages, but younger ones are easier to teach this. When we are only working for the reward, and not because we love what we do, then we are only motivated externally. Which usually, does not create the happiest life.

Internal motivation also teaches integrity, because we are not only doing it for the reward, but because we are proud to provide something of value. Integrity and value go hand in hand.

Work becomes like play when we do it with internal motivation.

Children also need lots of time to play and be creative with their endless imagination, so they do not feel overwhelmed and overworked. Getting too tired of something can destroy the excitement and motivation to finish the project. It is better for children to do a little bit every day, than working a full day with little play. Little by little, line upon line, precept upon precept. We need to remember how little they are, and not expect too much from them. Also not pressure them into perfection, less it destroys their motivation. Just make it a daily thing and a part of life, to get them to help, no matter what their age. It will pay off eventually.

External motivation is when we bribe, threaten, or force them to work. Or when we use fear, or guilt to pressure them into working. Work that they, otherwise, would not do. Yes, they will learn how to work through external motivation, but it can get to a point where they grow up and become workaholic to get away from the guilty feeling they get, as soon as they are not working. They beat themselves up and hardly know how to rest, relax, and refresh their bodies, causing them to get old quick. They find it hard to relax because of that guilty feeling that they should be doing something.

How can people that suffer from this 'work ethic' ever discover their authenticity, when they are governed by the training they received as a child? Yes, they make good workers, but what about their joy and happiness? Will they just slave to death and die prematurely?

Once they become parents, what will their children do when their parent never has time to play with them, or else feels guilty to play? Or never has time to let them help them with their work. This breeds a generation that will hate work, because work was more important to their parent than the children themselves.

The other side of the same coin is when parents that have been trained this way, now train their children the same way. Which just continues the slavery.

If we, as parents, have been forced to work when we were young, we may tend to feel like we can never do that to our children, and then we do not know how to get our children to work at all, which is not good, either.

When we have this problem, we first need to heal and reprogram ourselves. And realize that it is okay to take time off for our children and ourselves. And let go of the guilty feeling of our past training. Children need a balance. We all do. They need us to work with them, and also play with them. This is how intimate connections are made, and good relationships with our children become our reality.

Here is a real-life experience for an example:

My two-year-old daughter wanted to clean windows. My first thought was, 'Oh bother, she will only make a mess and will not do it right anyway.' (I was overwhelmed at the time) But then it hit me: If I want her to love doing work for me, I may not squash her willingness now. And I had to put my perfectionism behind me and realize what is important. And I decided that if I don't get something else done, because of how much it slowed me down, I will at least have planted a seed that I will be able to reap a harvest from, later in life.

And so, I provided her with the things she needed and showed her how, by doing the top windows she could not reach. As I watched her enjoying the bliss of helping me do something worthwhile, it gave me joy to realize that I made the most of the moment. After praising her for doing a good job, I realized how differently this situation could have turned out, and easily I could've crushed her willingness to help. And I realized that if I can continue to keep her inspired to help me, through her own motivation, that someday, I will have a big girl that loves helping me. She will love being with me if it turns out to be a pleasant experience, and I will have the opportunity to teach her everything I know, because she adores me and looks up to me with admiration.

3 years later, she is 5 and her favorite job is cleaning windows! And she is getting good at it, too!

How hard is it to teach children something, if they would rather be somewhere else, or want someone else for their teacher? Someone they would be more comfortable with. Someone who would not judge, correct, and criticize all the time, but love them unconditionally because of who they are. Someone who has a way of making a happy atmosphere.

How can we blame our children when they do not enjoy being with us? Can we take responsibility for ourselves without condemning ourselves and feel like failure? Can we still do something to change the situation?

The answer is, yes! It is never too late to practice respect and change ourselves, but it takes repentance and humbleness. And loving ourselves enough to forgive ourselves for past mistakes.

2. Responsibility

Giving our children responsibilities is important. It will grow their self-esteem and self-confidence.

When children feel needed with what they can contribute, it gives them a feeling of purpose.

Responsibilities should be easy enough that the children can do the task by themselves. And there should always be some fun things like feeding a pet.

When we give them too much responsibility and overwhelm them, they may feel like 'giving up', or feel the 'I can't' emotion. Children can be trained to say, "How can I?" instead of "I can't," but if they get the "I don't want to" attitude, or start grumbling, we should ask ourselves if we are overloading them. But we need to realize there may be other issues, too, that could be the reason for their 'I don't want to' attitude. When it is hard to figure out why they don't want to do something, one solution is to ask them in a kind and understanding manner, with respect. They may come out with an unexpected answer from which we can learn. There is always a reason behind children's behavior, and it is possible to figure it out, if we can humble ourselves enough to learn from them.

When we make a responsibility we give them, seem like an accomplishment, and praise them for it, it will boost their self-worth. But we need to be aware if they are doing it for approval only, or if they are doing it because it makes them feel good inside, which comes from a job well done.

Once we know, as a family, what each child is responsible for, then it becomes important that everyone is held accountable for their responsibility. Or else it is not their responsibility. When we, as parents, continue being responsible for reminding them, they will keep on depending on us to be responsible and making sure it gets done. When we do not hold them accountable, they can still blame us when something goes wrong or forgotten. And they can say, "Why didn't you tell me?"

But when they cannot depend on us for it, then automatically, they will have no one to blame but themselves, when something does not get done. They will try hard not to let it happen again, thus becoming responsible children.

3. Teamwork

To have our family live and work together in harmony as a team, we need to know each child's personality type, so we know where they fit best. What is worse than trying to make a lion be an elephant? Each can do wonderful things, but they need to be respected for who they are and what they can do best.

If we have a 'born leader' type, then we need to give that child leadership responsibilities at a young age, so we channel his strengths where they will be most appreciated.

If we have a 'supportive' type, we need to show our child appreciation for his/her supportive ways and encourage him/her to be their best self.

If we have a creative child that is always coming up with new and strange ideas, it is important to let them try out their ideas, realistic or not. And we need to let them take their toys apart if they want to figure out how they work.

Children are happier when they may contribute something of value that they came up with and are good at, naturally. It is important that children feel good in their own skin, which is called self-acceptance. If they can have respect for their body and talents and be grateful for who they are, and love themselves and their talents, then they are naturally better team members. Because if they love and respect themselves, they can love and respect others. When they can feel good with who they are, they can readily accept others, too.

Vice versa, if they are not satisfied with themselves, they will not be satisfied with others, either. We will hear them complaining about others and picking fights a lot more.

Us, as human beings, naturally want to experience life with each other. None of wants to be lonely. We all want to be part of a team, something bigger than ourselves. Because together we can accomplish more. We designed to co-create.

The reason we feel like isolating ourselves, is because we have been hurt in the past, and it is now hard to trust others. We all have some kind of reason to be hurt, but that does not mean we have to stay hurt. Healing is possible, when we choose to let go of the past and forgive.

When little children fall and hurt themselves, we give them love and expect them to heal and return to their normal state of happiness. Which is how we should all be able to.

But, what if we do not get the love we need to heal from a trauma? Then that part of our system shuts down, so we do not need to feel the pain anymore, even though it is still there. If we have any unhealed traumas that need to be loved so they can heal, then it is up to us, to love that hurting part of ourselves, so we can move on with our life, and experience joy once again. We do not need to wait on anyone else to love us. If we wait on others to love us, we could be waiting for the rest of our life.

We can take responsibility for our own healing and become better team members in our adult life, thus creating an example for our children how to be good teammates.

When we all work together, play together, sing together, When we all eat together, how happy we'll be.....When your work is my work and our work is God's work, When we all work together, how happy we'll be...

4. Creativity

Creativity does not need to be taught to most children. It is something that needs to be allowed and encouraged. If we, as parents, struggle with being creative, then we can let children or other people teach us how to be creative. We are naturally born to create, but maybe our creativity got destroyed when we were yet children, and we became conditioned to always do what others think up for us, instead of getting ideas from within ourselves. There is always time to rebuild our creativity by opening our minds and let go of what others think. We can still learn how much power our brain has, to give us new ideas, when we can just 'let go' and let our creativity flow.

By helping our children with their creative ideas, it can reprogram our brains into a creative state of mind. It is important that we give them time, space, and materials to create their own ideas, so they have what they need. Yet it does not take much.

Being creative makes children independent. When children are left to find something to do on their own, it will probably be something creative. When we let our children have the space and freedom to create and think for themselves, they can come up with unique ways of entertaining themselves, requiring less toys and less of our time. Free, uninterrupted time is a bonus for us, as parents, because we all need a break at times.

Creative children are less demanding, because they entertain themselves. When we always provide entertainment, they become dependent on outside sources for entertainment, which is destructive in later years.

How can they come up with their own uniqueness, when we are constantly giving them more than they can handle, or shoving stuff at them before they are ready? It is beneficial for children to be bored sometimes, because that is a time when they can think and daydream. Times of stillness is key to brainstorming new ideas. Being creative, requires mental thinking, and is good for healthy brain development. We need to be careful to not criticize their creative ideas, less they get discouraged and never try it again. As long as they are not doing harm with their creations, and it is safe. Complimenting their ideas, inspires them to do more, and become even better and smarter.

If we want our children to grow up and be better people than what we, their parents, are, one solution is to let them be creative. When we let them be creative and encourage creativity, they may come up with things we have never taught them, which is good. That is how the world becomes a better place, when new generations are allowed to create new things and better ways of doing things. Things that will make us proud to be their parents.

It all starts when they are small and are encouraged to be creative.

# 5

# Repetition

Children are like wet clay, mold-able to anyway we train them. They are being conditioned and molded every minute they live with us. Anything can be taught through repetition. Doing something over and over trains a brain, no matter what age. Even animals have the ability to learn when something gets done over and over.

Our way of life is repetition, over and over. How can children be anything different than their parents? Children are great imitators. They look to example and watch how others do things, then they try it themselves. Children are easy to teach before they get the 'I know better than you' attitude.

Us older folks tend to have a lot of resistance to learning new things and making the necessary changes that it takes to get the results we are looking for. It is much harder to retrain a brain than it is to teach a little child something new. But that does not say that it is impossible. It just takes a lot of patience and understanding, with love for ourselves.

It is easy for children to learn this happy way of life. If we can let them teach us, we are learning from some of the best teachers out there. They can see things as they really are in a simple, uncomplicated way. Many amazing things have come out of the mouth of babes.

Children are good at knowing how honest we are. They can sense if we are being real and authentic with them, or if we have this inflated, 'I know better than you' attitude. When we can open mindedly ask their opinion on a specific issue that they can understand, they may come up with a surprisingly simple solution. Maybe it is something we did not want to hear or admit, but deep down, we know it is the truth. And it might be the answer we need.

Children's perspective on life is different from us adults because they are less confused. Being humble enough to admit that we do not know everything, and asking them for their honest opinion, goes a long way in building a good relationship with our children. It gives them validation and is good for their autonomy. Just knowing that they have a voice and that their opinion matters, creates self-confidence and a healthy self-esteem. It also creates space for camaraderie, because it feels like we are all in this boat together, living and learning together. It also gives them space to fail without judgment and try again, when they see us do it and it becomes a normal, healthy way of life.

When we fail, who is quicker to forgive, than a child? Is it hard to admit we made a mistake and ask forgiveness from our children? Just because we are older than our children, does not mean our souls are wiser. All wisdom comes from within, and they have just as much access to it (if not more), than we do. Because their minds do not interfere with it, the way our programmed, damaged minds do.

If we can admit to our children when we were wrong, and say

'I'm sorry,' then it becomes easy to connect with our children again. Our vulnerability makes them feel like they are not the only ones making mistakes. And it makes it easier for them to apologize when they make mistakes.

Once we can all realize that it is okay to make mistakes, and to be less than perfect, then we can relax and enjoy the moments more with our children, as they grow so quickly. It is through our trial and errors that we all learn the lessons in life and that is perfectly okay. Having this mindset, gives our children freedom to learn and grow naturally.

# 6

# Teaching our Children How to Connect with God Within Themselves

Or change it around and let our children teach us how to connect with God within ourselves

Maybe they know how to do it, that we are not aware of it. Children under age six are more connected, before they get distracted by society. Can we teach our children how to connect with God, if we are not living out that connection?

Remember: More is caught than taught

Heartfelt prayer or meditation is one way to connect with God, Jesus, Source, Universe, Energy, Love, or whatever term each one calls this Life Producer.

Gratitude is another way to open the channels and gateways to this Higher Power

Connecting to God is as easy as breathing. We just need to go inside the room of our heart where our breath is, to find God. This is where we meet the Divine Power, which is called Life. Open the doors and let the Love shine out. God is Love and is as simple as that. Wherever we find Love, we find God. This Love Energy is also the Healing Energy that heals all diseases.

Just open the doors and let the Love out. Breathe deeply. As you breathe in gratitude, breathe out Love. Let the Love pour out to others around you, until it gushes out like an unstoppable river, cleaning out all the stagnation within.

Find out what you love to do, because that is your God-given purpose in this life. Eat the foods you love and enjoy them to the fullest and they will heal you, because Love heals. Foods we crave, can be different than foods we love.

When we love the body God has created and given to us, then naturally, Love is flowing through, and it becomes healed and aligned. It is His temple, and it is where he lives and has His Being. We are created in His image and are One with Him. There is no need to look outside ourselves, as though we are separate from God, because He lives within. Children know this through instinct, till they get conditioned to believe something else. Which is why Jesus likened the Kingdom of God to the little children, and why He said, "The Kingdom of Heaven is within.

Teaching our children gratitude by example, is a great way to show them how to connect to God, because gratitude opens the gateway to Heaven, and the Kingdom of Heaven is within.

Practicing gratitude and feeling grateful is different from saying "Thank-you" for good manners or showing respect. Saying "thank-you" out of obligation or habit does not bring connection unless it is felt.

As I questioned and searched my heart for answers on why we must make our children say "Thank-you", so others do not judge us or get offended, I felt God was about to teach me something important. And I wondered if we know what gratefulness truly means. Do we just practice it to make a show of it?

If we want our children to feel grateful for what they receive, we must be that example. Do we expect them to feel gratitude when they hear us complain about things? Children are great imitators. They will automatically be grateful for everything, when they live in an environment of gratitude and hear it all the time. What we see in our children is a reflection of ourselves and our habits.

So, for me, I had some gratitude to practice first, before I could expect my children to just feel grateful and bubble out gratefulness when they receive something. I needed to show them how I felt when they gave me something or did something for me. Or about the beautiful day outside, or the rain that makes the flowers and food grow in the garden.

It did not take long for my children to notice and start copying me. One time, I asked my three-year-old how he feels about something I gave him, and he at once responded, "Thank-You!" And I knew it came from deep within and not just because I wanted him to say it. Right then I knew that I found my answer.

How can we feel grateful and not be connected to God? Gratitude comes from within. Praying without ceasing is breathing in gratitude and breathing out Love which keeps us connected to God continuously. Every word we say, becomes a prayer when we live in love with our body that God created for Himself to live in and have His Being. Every breath we take, is Life from the Love inside.

We just need to learn how to let the love out and let it overflow like a fountain, to bless others. It is as simple as breathing deeply and fully and knowing that all things work together for good to them that love God. Relax in the peace of stillness and the knowing that God is here, and all is well. Then it becomes easy to feel appreciation for life itself and all the beauty that surrounds us daily, for us to enjoy while we live on this beautiful planet named Earth. Every moment becomes a wonderful moment.

# 7

# What is Manipulation?

Manipulation is a form of control.

Here are 4 common mistakes parents make and they are all manipulation.

1. Bribing
2. Threatening
3. Making false promises
4. Punishing instead of disciplining

These are four ways that we, as a society, have been programmed and taught how to do. It is the reason our human society is like it is now. To change our world and solve it's problems, we need to understand why it became this way and how to do differently, so we can make the change within ourselves and our homes first. We need to be the example and show others how. And keep on learning how to become better than we were yesterday.

When we search for answers, we will find answers. In this chapter, we will uncover some answers on why these four ways continue to destroy relationships between parents and children.

## WHAT IS MANIPULATION?

The other side of the same coin is to 'give in' and let our children do whatever they want. And then we will have the problem of our children manipulating us and we need to cater to their every wish and fantasy to avoid some kind of meltdown. Because now the children are in control and the parents must obey if they do not want a fight. This also destroy relationships and breeds disrespect.

Where is the sweet spot of enforcing boundaries or rules, yet keep the relationships blooming and promoting deep respect?

First, we need to respect ourselves, before we can expect others to respect us.

Remember: Respect is something that needs to be earned for it to last.

Respect is the answer to end manipulation. If we respect ourselves, we will naturally be respectful to our children and others, and in return our children and others will respect us.

Children imitate what they see being done. How can we expect our children to be any different than we are? If we do not like what we see in our children, the only way to make a lasting, positive change, is to change ourselves.

Why do parents blame their children when things turn out wrong in their families? Can we take responsibility for what we create?

It may not be our fault for the way we have been trained and molded, but it is our responsibility to change and heal ourselves if we want to create a better future for our children and grandchildren. No one can change our life for us. It is up to us. But even we cannot make a change unless we find out the why's and the how's.

In our times today, we have everything available at our fingertips with technology, including the knowledge of how to change and create better futures.

"Ignorance is bliss", they say, but choosing to stay ignorant is choosing hardship for the future.

To change, requires us to get out of our comfort level, which is never easy. But it is necessary if we ever want to make a difference in our life and the lives of other people. Let us take heart and be brave.

Now we are ready to look at these four ways of manipulation and see some examples of how we do this.

1.Bribing

This is a common way to get children to do something they do not want to do. Promising them a reward, so they would get it done. It is motivating them from the outside, which is called external motivation. Bribing may work at first, but as time goes on, the rewards need to be increased, to keep them motivated. And it will become harder and harder to get them to do something, because it will not feel worth it to them if it is not exciting or motivating enough. They have become so dependent on rewards, that now they refuse to do anything without a significant reward. They become demanding, selfish, and unappreciative. It makes them feel like they deserve everything. It becomes a real problem in adulthood.

For example: The room needs to be cleaned up. They already know it, but since they were not promised a reward, why bother? It becomes harder and harder to keep the room clean. Since they are not internally motivated, (meaning they 'want' to keep their room clean), they are incapable of doing it unless someone motivates them.

To change this around, we need to first ask ourselves, "How neat are we? How often, and how well do we clean up after ourselves? Are we internally motivated to keep our house neat?"

If we are not, we may be dealing with the result of how we have been trained when we were young.

Or, the other side of the same coin, where we have been forced into being neat, and now we feel frustrated or guilty as soon as it gets a little messy. And we project it unto our children if we do not heal ourselves.

In either circumstance, we need to check the reality of being neat. Are we neat because of what others think, or are we neat because of how it makes us feel, or do we not care if we are neat or not?

Once we realize the value of being neat and cleaning up after ourselves, then we help our children understand how much better it is to be neat. And we can help them appreciate the value of living in a neat space. Naturally, they will love and appreciate what we do. And with help and encouragement, they will gladly and willingly help us clean the room. And by and by, they will do it by themselves without being reminded, because they have been trained to do it.

An important thing to remember is this: Children love working side by side with someone they love to be with.

Then someday they will be proud to master it by themselves and surprise us when they come to us proudly and say, "Did you notice how clean my room is?"

That is personal accomplishment and should be praised to encourage more of that.

Another thing to be aware of, is to not expect perfection, but strive to become better and better. It is important to give ourselves grace when we do not get the room cleaned up, or our house neat all the time. Seeing the opposite of neatness every now and then, makes us realize the value of neatness and motivates us to stay neat. It is not about being perfect, but to make our life enjoyable, so we can live it out to the fullest potential.

Bribing also increases the chances of our children giving up, because the reward does not exceed the hardship of doing the task, so why bother?

Bribing demotivates and reduces curiosity. They merely do it for the reward that we offered, instead of the value of doing the task.

2. Threatening

A threat is a phrase of something bad, to put enough fear into the person we want to manipulate.

If we need to put fear into our children to get them to do what we want, then that is proof that we do not have their respect, which is deep admiration. Respect needs to be earned. We can never force our children to respect us. They will either fear us, respect us, or disrespect us.

When we threaten our children, they start doubting our unconditional love. They start mistrusting and it follows them into future relationships.

We become a threat and they become afraid, which is the opposite of what we want. We want them to know and feel that we love them unconditionally. We want them to be able to trust us, so they confide their deepest fears and longings to us.

If we love them based on their actions, then our love becomes conditional. Children are sensitive and know distinctly what true love is, and whether they are getting it, or not. They behave accordingly, and show us if they get what they need, or do not get what they need.

This is key to having well-behaved children. The key is how well they feel loved.

Unruly behavior always stems from some kind of deep-rooted

issue. As long as those deep roots do not get up-rooted, we will keep on getting the same results. Once we look below the surface and find out the why and how, we will be able to come up with a solution.

When we start listening to our children, they may tell us what we need to know, which will give us clues to finding our answer.

Threats always produce negative results. Children produce outward compliance through fear, but it is not the way to a good future relationship with our children. Using threats as means of control ignites the longing to jump from our ship at the first opportunity when they are old enough. Then the parents wonder where they missed it with them.

Threatening children can damage parts of their system for life if they never discover how to heal themselves.

For example: When a child refuses to eat a particular food and the child gets threatened. The child may or may not eat it. In either case, that particular food can become bad tasting to this child for the rest of his/her life. Every time after that, just the sight or smell of that particular food will cause a negative reaction, a bad memory and something to stay away from.

If we, as adults, went through this scenario as a child, we will be able to remember that feeling of disgust and hate for that particular food.

4. Punishing

There is a difference between punishing and discipline, which will be explained in a later chapter.

The punishing that harms a child, is what is being referred to right here. The punishing that gets done out of anger and frustration. It makes children afraid and angry. It encourages them to lie every chance they get, to escape punishment.

Many of us, as parents, know the fear of getting punished

when we were yet children. Society has taught us that this is the way we make our children behave. It works for the moment, but rebellion grows out of being used harshly and unfairly.

Nowadays, there are many sad parents and grandparents who are confused why their children and grandchildren stay away. Lots of parents do not know why their children grew up and went ways of which they did not approve.

Children that have been raised up in fear, instead of respect, will not respect their parents, nor ask for advice once they are ready to be on their own.

Punishing our children because they do not conform to our control and manipulation, hurts our relationship with our children. Because their emotions are hurt and misunderstood, it makes them afraid of us afterward. Neither will they be able to trust us as someone safe to tell their innermost longings and struggles. If the 'control' continues as children become teenagers, the gap becomes wider and wider between parents and their children. The parents wonder why their children never ask them for advice or direction. And why the children want to be wherever their parents are not.

Children have an inner knowing of what is right or wrong, good or evil. They know if they are loved unconditionally and respected as a human being. They know if they are misunderstood and abused and will behave accordingly. Instinct tells them they have rights, till parents or teachers convince them that they do not have a voice or choice. They either 'rebel', or 'give in' to avoid conflict.

Then later parents wonder why their children do not speak up or cannot say what they want to say. And wonder why their children seem irritated, sad, or angry. Anger comes from being hurt in the past.

It is important to not provoke our children to wrath.

These 4 common mistakes that parents make, all come from reaction. When we take the time to think before we act, and realize that we could do differently, then we could act differently, because our hearts would come up with a better solution.

Parents also wonder why their children look to forbidden things in life for fulfillment. Children keep looking for ways of finding happiness and joy, because they did not get it when they were little. It may lead them into the trap of addiction, all because they are trying to fill up the emptiness inside. Or trying to numb themselves from the pain of the past, because they do not know how to deal with it.

It is hard to undo the past for parents that have teens like this, but it does not have to be undone. With enough sincere apologies in word and deed, and with changed hearts, relationships can be repaired, healed, and restored for better future relationships.

# 8

# What is the Difference?

1. What is the difference between punishment and discipline?
2. What is the difference between rewards and incentives or the difference between bribing or training with boundaries?

First, we will look at the difference between punishment and discipline.

Punishment is usually done in anger, and it creates fear. Dictators use punishment for control, because fear is effective to control others. Punishment often comes after a threat. Threatening a child is mental abuse and harmful.

Discipline is correction with love. It is training and guidance, leading towards the right direction.

Children naturally want to be good and do what is right. When they have done wrong, it is a relief, when they receive discipline to relieve them from guilt. They feel better when a parent loves them enough to correct their wrongdoing and set them in the right direction in a loving way. Connecting with our children before we correct them, makes a bigger impact.

Connecting with our children builds respect, and they will want to copy our ways when they admire us.

On the other hand, when children do wrong, and they feel guilty and bad about themselves and what they did, then to make it worse, they get hurt emotionally by an angry parent. This only makes them angry, instead of releasing their guilt. Being told how bad they are, now gives them reason to believe that about themselves. And the anger that arose from being punished harshly fuels the negative feelings. The punishment has put fear and mistrust in their hearts, and now they feel unloved and hurt mentally and physically. The anger now brings on more bad behavior, creating a downward spiral. Lying becomes a habit, to try and avoid more pain. And the gulf between parents and children become harder and harder to bridge. It makes children do the opposite of what they are being taught.

Children naturally want to be good people. We all do, and especially children at a young age, before they get damaged. Little children are pure, till parents and teachers imprint the ways of the world on them. No wonder Jesus likened the Kingdom of Heaven unto the little children.

When they get hurt often enough, neglected, and misunderstood, then they start behaving in a way that draws attention and they also try to protect themselves, which is where lying starts. They lie because they are afraid of what would happen if they told the truth.

We want our children to trust us and feel safe to tell us their innermost thoughts. It is how they will learn how to trust God. Do we expect them to trust God if they cannot trust their own parents? Children view God the same way they see their parents.

Children will all make mistakes and that is okay. That is how each of us learn in life, through experiencing our own mistakes. And if we traumatize them, because they did something we considered wrong, (which may have been a great opportunity to learn from), then they will learn something. They will learn that we are not always understanding and that our love is conditional. They know that we are bigger than them for now, but they will be waiting for the day when they can be on their own. It will have molded them.

Then later parents wonder why their children seem so distant and inside themselves, don't care about them, and just feel better and happier without them.

Training children's wills is different from breaking their wills. To break their wills is to break their spirits. To train, is to mold and guide them, so that they willingly do what we want, without being forced.

Children can feel instinctively when we have their best interest in mind, and they know if we truly love them.

2. What is the difference between rewards and incentives or the difference between bribing and training with boundaries?

Bribing children with rewards destroys internal motivation. Paying rewards breeds entitlement. Rewards manipulate them into doing something they normally wouldn't. Children become dependent on external pressure and motivation to get into action. And they become less curious.

Rewards are the easy way out for parents who do not feel like investing themselves into making it fun working together.

Incentives, on the other hand, are all about winning the game. It is enjoying the challenge of the game, while competing, then celebrating together in the end.

Incentives are the why, how, and the joy of action and doing.

Having fun doing something challenging with someone who cares about them. Children should never be left to do a big task by themselves, lest they get discouraged.

If they voluntarily do a big task by themselves for a surprise, then that is a different story.

Children learn a good work ethic if they can work alongside someone bigger and get the job done before they get too tired and feel like giving up.

When they feel forced or manipulated to work, then they resent it and will not learn how to love working. Because then they are only doing it out of pressure, of guilt, of fear, and not from internal motivation. Internal motivation is where the joy comes from.

A 'work ethic' that comes out of pressure, is not good, even when the work gets done well, because the main ingredients are missing, which are joy and purpose.

Enforcing boundaries means to make boundaries and then stand on them, not letting our children push us over. It is about respecting ourselves. When we speak with firmness, so that they know there is no use arguing, or throwing a fit, then we can enforce boundaries without harming them. (more will be explained in a later chapter on how to do this) Because in the end, whatever we say, goes, when we do not give in.

5. Giving in

'Giving in' is the fifth common mistake that parents make. When we give in to our children's whining, we are letting them control and manipulate us. If they can throw a tantrum and it works, then they will use that tactic to get their way. If it works to grumble, then they will become grumblers when we assign them work or try to make boundaries.

It takes strong people to say 'No.' But saying 'No' is necessary when we make boundaries and stand our ground. Making boundaries, and then giving in because we cannot say 'No', makes it confusing to children. Or, if we did not make it clear what we expect, makes it confusing as well.

Children are happier when they know boundaries and the boundaries stay enforced, meaning there is no option to try pushing the lines. Firm, strong boundaries promote respect and security. No boundaries, or half-kept boundaries, promote disrespect and insecurity.

# 9

# How Often Do We Hurt Our Children Unconsciously?

1. Children's feelings are particularly important.

When we misunderstand our children, their feelings get hurt. Just like we all do when we look for validation.

And if we do not make it right, their trust in us will decline.

For us to understand our children's needs, we need to be educated on how human beings operate and feel, including ourselves. Which can be quite the journey, but it is worth it.

Remember, they are just like us, only smaller.

2. When we shove them away and do not want to be bothered. When we are too busy, they will begin to feel unimportant and unworthy.

Exceptions are: When they beforehand know not to interrupt us in the moment, and they know that we will be there for them after we are done.

It is important for us parents to have some uninterrupted 'me-time' each day, and equally important to also give the children some quality time and love each day. Like doing something fun with them, or just listen what they have to say. This builds respect for each other.

3. When there is stress between Father and Mother, it makes the child feel unsafe and afraid.

Children absorb these feelings and make them their own, feeling like it is their fault. It brings along guilt and shame which makes them feel shy and uncertain of themselves when in a group of people. They grow up and continue searching for the love that was not present in their life. They have an inner knowing that they need love. Absence of love makes an emptiness inside, which is the reason many people struggle with addictions and poor lifestyle habits. Because they are trying to fill the emptiness inside, they keep on searching for more.

The entire world needs compassion and understanding, and most of all, Love.

For us to make a difference in the world, we first need to find out how to love and be loved personally, by ourselves, so we can heal. And so we can love our spouses, our children, our neighbors, our community, and so we can love the whole world and all humanity on it. How can we love unconditionally, if we do not know what unconditional love is?

The most important step is to discover how to be filled to overflowing with Love, so it can overflow to everyone we interact with.

4. Taking away children's freedom, hurts them at a deep core level. Control and force are the strongest ways we can cripple them. Their rights as a human being, are to be free, be creative, think for themselves, have choices, and be respected.

We, as adults with more experience, are here to lead, guide and protect them. We are not here to take away their freedom. We are here to prepare them the best we know how to go on their own when they reach the age of adulthood.

If we have to say 'No' to something, it should be explained why to the best of our knowledge.

We are not Lords over our children, and they are not ours to keep. We have the privilege of holding their little hands, only a small part of their entire life. We are assigned to be their guardians. They are co-creators with us. Co-creators of harmony and peace. All humans are created equal.

Children naturally want to please us when they feel loved, respected, and secure. Someday they will be the driver, taking care of us, if they stick around. 5. Labeling our children limits them and makes them believe that is who they are. It puts them in a box and keeps them from being authentic.

They live up to what we believe of them. So for example, If we often tell them they are sloppy, they will be sloppy, and soon they will be able to excuse themselves and say, "Well, we are just sloppy kids." Because that's how they believe they are. It keeps them taking responsibility and become better

When we have a habit of saying, "You are bad!", they will be bad to match that belief. To say, "That thing they did was bad," already puts it in a different perspective, because now it is not them that is bad, but the thing they did, which can be left in the past.

Being real with our children and speaking life into them is the way to teach them authenticity. Praise them for their good behavior to encourage more of that, then when disturbing behavior happens, then figure out where it is coming from and why. Talk to them in a connected, understanding way, which is how we get the results we want.

6. Blaming our children for our emotional upsets like anger. Yes, our children will trigger us and we will get angry if, we have unresolved trauma.

But if we blame them for our anger, instead of going within and healing that trauma, then they will grow up feeling like it is their fault. A guilt-laden child is not a happy child.

Blaming someone else for our emotional state, will only keep us stuck and will never fix anything. We are not taking responsibility if we play the blame game.

If we want a happy life, we need to heal our childhood traumas and let them go, then move on to a brighter future.

# 10

# Creating Harmony in The Home

1. [2]Earn your children's respect
2. Make respected boundaries
3. Plan in advance and create a routine and rhythm that works for your family
4. Listen to your children and empathize with them
5. Understand your family's needs and your own
6. Be the example and practice the Golden Rule

This chapter is the conclusion of this book, finalizing the answers and focusing on what we need to do moving forward, now that we have become aware of the common mistakes parents make and have more clarity where bad behavior stems from.

1. Earn your children's respect

Having our children's respect, needs to be priority if we expect them to want to please us. Respect is admiration, so that means

---

[2]

we need to be admirable.

For our family to respect us, we need to be respectable. We need to respect our own needs as well as their needs. We need to live our life with integrity and love, so we are someone worth imitating. We need to treat ourselves and our children as people worthy of respect.

Listening to each other is respecting each other's feelings and opinions.

Practicing the Golden Rule shows respect to others

Letting go of control and the attitude of 'I'm better than you', makes it easier to be respectful

Being real and honest, and just being our true authentic selves, with no pressure to be who someone else thinks we should be, is a big step into respecting and loving ourselves. Finding out what we are created to do and discovering our true purpose, lights up our whole life, and as we continue to move forward into our joy, respect comes naturally.

2. Make respected boundaries

Making boundaries is essential if we want our family to respect each other. Each family member needs their personal space that no one else has a say over. When we let our little children have their own space and rights, they will never have a problem making boundaries. Then it is also important to keep them responsible to keep their space neat.

It is harder for us adults to learn how to make boundaries, if we have been trained to be self-less, and we feel guilty as soon as we do something for ourselves. If we have been so trained to always give and always serve others and do what everyone wants, then we have become a slave to society. This eventually leads to burnout, if we do not learn how to take care of ourselves and recharge.

Being a parent requires lots of selflessness, but if we do not know how to respect ourselves and make sure we are taken care of, we will eventually burn out and not be able to take care of anyone. We will feel used, unappreciated, and disrespected.

Once we learn how to make boundaries and respect ourselves enough to enforce and keep those boundaries, then our lives can become harmonious. Because now everyone can recharge and we all have more to give, out of our abundance of energy and overflowing love.

At first, when we start making boundaries, we may not be very good at keeping them tight, but as soon as we let our children push our boundaries around, we will experience less peace and harmony. There will be confusion where the boundaries belong, which can make it frustrating to the point where we explode or crash, because we have been pushed around. That just tells us that we have not been firm enough with our 'No'. We do not need to argue or fight about it, just saying "NO" firmly, is all it takes. In the end, if we are the parent and we are the biggest, then whatever we say, goes, right?

Involving our children in the process of making boundaries and rules, makes them feel included. And if we can explain the purpose of each rule and boundary, it makes it clearer to them why, and they will be able to remember it and respect the boundary more.

For example: Mother needs a nap and some quiet time. The boundary could be a sign on the bedroom door, "Do Not Disturb". If the children know what the sign means and know why they cannot go in, then they will be able to respect the sign. If we can explain to them that we can be a better mother when we take a nap, and then give them something quiet to do, to keep them occupied, they will be happy to accommodate us. They will be looking forward to seeing us refreshed and energized again. All children love when their parents feel good.

If we wait till we are at the end of our tolerance level, then we are forced to quickly go in our room and shut the door with no time for explaining before we explode, then our children can feel hurt, confused, neglected and pushed back. And if we explode first and lash out at them because we cannot take it anymore, that is harmful, too. And this brings us to the third part.

3. Plan in advance and create a routine and rhythm that works for your family

To plan in advance, we need to have a clear picture in our mind what we want our family life to look like. Once we know what we want, then we can talk with our children and spouse about what we would like to see happen. We need to get them excited and ask them for their ideas and insights on how to get our family in a state of peace and harmony, and they may come up with surprisingly good ideas. They will feel honored and respected to be included in the decisions.

Remember: Having a family is having a team and it is not just about ourselves. Doing things together in teamwork, is what creates harmony, which is the sole purpose of this book.

Here is an important key to keep in mind, too. If not everyone is having fun, then it is not fun. This is about making sure each family member has a voice, a choice, and space to feel part of the group. It is about making sure each person is respected and living their best life. Because if one person feels left out, unusable, and unhappy, then we cannot function as a complete group.

Does that mean we can just exclude the one person and continue without them?

For example: How does an engine work if one part is missing

or broken? What do we do if an engine breaks down and has no more power?

We stop and get it fixed, because that is the only option if we ever want to use that engine again.

Same with children. If one person or child in the group is not co-operating, it is a sign that something needs to be fixed. It means they are asking for help. And if we have love and respect, we will ask them what they need, and listen, and then do what it takes to get all the parts working again.

Sometimes an engine needs to be overhauled and worked on extensively, if all the parts need attention. And that is okay if takes a while. We need to be patient with ourselves and others when there is a lot of healing to be done before we can move forward. We need to keep our focus on the end result, which is a fully functioning family, moving forward with the power of love, being able to bless everyone we interact with, in endless harmony. It is possible, because with God, (which is Love), nothing is impossible.

Having a routine and rhythm is also important in establishing harmony in the home. When children know what's what, they will be happier and feel safer. Then we also need to give them options within the limit.

For example: If we make a set time to be in bed by evening, then we can let them decide in what order they want to do their bedtime routine, like brush their teeth, wash themselves, bedtime snack, bedtime story, prayers, hugs, and so on.

Letting the children know beforehand what they can expect, eliminates tantrums, because it gives them time to think over it, and prepare to do it. They do not feel controlled, when they have time to willingly get ready.

Our rules and boundaries should never be so strict that there are no exceptions to the rule. If we can always be understanding of the situation, then the children will feel loved and secure. It is not about being perfect, it is about having peace and harmony in our home, where our bodies can relax, recharge, and make many happy memories together.

4. Listen to the children and empathize with them.

Listening to what our children are saying, means looking into their beautiful eyes, and feel what they are trying to say. Feeling the emotion behind their eyes, means everything to them. Fully understanding and remembering how it felt to be a child, goes a long way in building trust and respect.

Our children are human beings, just like us. Their bodies have not grown to our size, but that does not mean their souls are not equal to our souls. We are eternal, divine Beings, and are called God's children. We are made in His likeness and created in His image. Our souls have come to earth to experience Life in human bodies, learning how to integrate and grow. Let us have compassion for each other and ourselves.

It is so good to remember how we felt as a child when something needs to be addressed. But sometimes our children experience things we never have. Then we can still try to put ourselves in their little shoes and try to imagine how they may be feeling, and at least try to understand. And it is okay to admit that we do not know how they feel and that we have a hard time understanding. At least they know we tried, and we care, and that is what matters.

It is also important to not just pity them but help them get back in their happy state. Pity is poison if we help them wallow in it. But listening to them, helps them to release, so they can move on.

People that have no one to listen to them, have a challenge of releasing the pain. Then it stays and keeps hurting instead of healing. Everyone needs a listening ear now and then. We are not meant to carry our heartaches and pains by ourselves, but nor is it okay to project them unto others. It is important that we learn how to 'let go' and surrender to what is, which can be done through gratitude. Being grateful for the hard things in life, allows us to release and learn from our experiences, then move on to better days and more challenges to overcome.

Growing, evolving, and emerging victorious, is what this life is all about. Every caterpillar must first crawl, then be wrapped in a dark cocoon before it can emerge into a beautiful butterfly.

So cling to the hope of better days, when all is dark, and you feel stuck and wrapped in a shell. When it is time, we will scratch out of our cocoon, if we wait with patience and never give up.

Someday we will have a story to share to inspire others if we keep on keeping on. Having the winning attitude is what gets people successful. Those who seek will find.

5. Understand your family's needs and your own

This is important if we want harmony. We all have the same needs on a physical level. The human species operate the same all around the globe.

Yet, we are also individuals that are all different from each other. None of us are exactly alike, which is why we need to accept each other as unique. And respect each other as individuals, rather than a herd of cattle, all crowded together in one herd.

A body has many different parts to it. The different parts all have different functions. How silly would it be if the hands would think they need to do what the feet are designed to do? Or the liver would think it needs to pump blood, because that is what the heart is doing? What if the eyes would feel bad because they cannot hear like the ears can?

That is silly, but that is what us humans do when we compare ourselves with others and think we need to behave like someone else. We are each designed to do something special and unique. Something that no one can do exactly like we can.

We are all part of one body, one unity, making it possible for the Earth to go around. Nobody is better than another just because we have different assignments. Is our stomach not as important as the brain, because the brain has the important job of telling the rest of the body how to operate? That is silly, because everyone knows that the brain is of no use to the stomach if the stomach is not there. And the stomach does not know how to function without the brain.

The point here is that we all need each other. None of us is complete in ourselves. We are all part of the whole, of the oneness of God. Everywhere we go, every day we are using things someone else has created and contributed. How much would we have in this life if we would have only that which we have created? Would we have anything? Because the material we use to create something was created by someone beforehand. All raw materials come from Mother Earth, God, the Universe, Energy, Source, which is the Oneness that we all live by as we take each breath. Can we comprehend how much we much we co-create and need each other to survive?

That is why we are commanded to love one another as ourselves, because we are all of the One. There is no use trying to move on without each other, no use separating ourselves from the One, for then we will perish. We rise together, or we rise none.

But even though we function as a collective, we also each function uniquely, which means that we all have unique talents, purposes, and needs. We need to discover our own uniqueness, so we can do our part with purpose in such a time as this. And then help our children discover their uniqueness, so they can be happy and therefore prosperous as they grow. And help them get started sharing their gifts and value with others.

6. Be the example and practice the Golden Rule

This last one is alone one of the biggest secrets to having a harmonious relationship with our children.

Do Unto Others as You Would Have Them Do Unto You

Maybe it is the BEST secret on raising children. It fixes so many things and eliminates so many problems. If this whole book would be focused on this one thing, would anything else be necessary?

Understanding the why's of life's problems are also important, but it still boils down to this point.

How beautifully everyone would work together in all aspects of life if this would be practiced all the time, all throughout the world, through all ages! No wonder it is called the Golden Rule, because it is Golden!

If we can master this Rule in our marriages, then our families, then our communities, and then the entire world can change!

Let's do this! Cheers!!!




Note from the author:

Please leave a review on Amazon so I can learn how to better serve the people as I write more books. Thank you! Here is the link: https://a.co/d/bsv01AP

www.ingramcontent.com/pod-product-compliance
Lightning Source LLC
Chambersburg PA
CBHW022120090426
42743CB00008B/935